Words of Love

Let's create our stories of love.

PRADEEPTI RANJAN

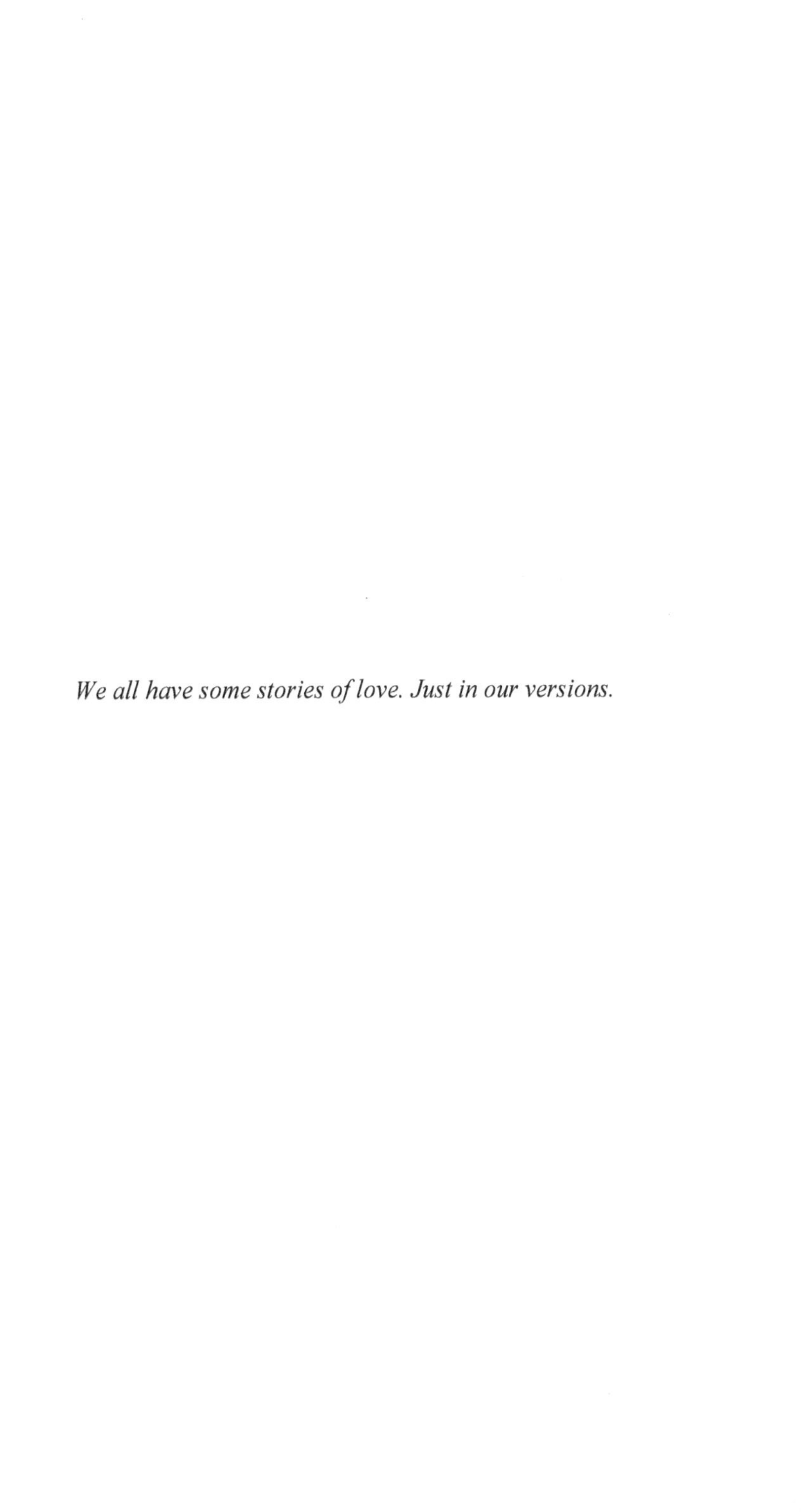

We all have some stories of love. Just in our versions.

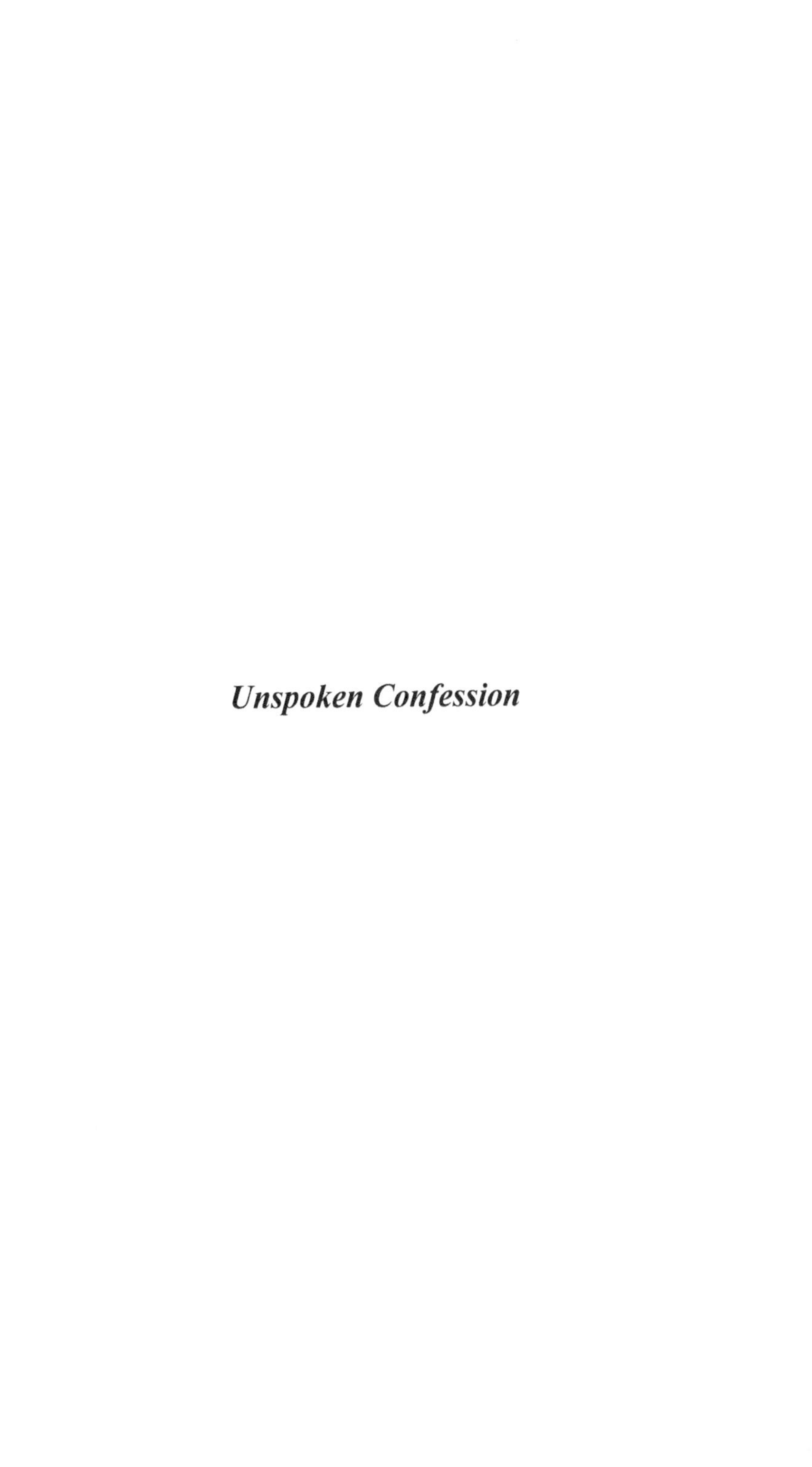

Unspoken Confession

Stories of eternity, our love will never disappear

In each other's arms, our hearts are serenely swayed

Eternal entangled, our souls so profound

Tales of forever, a passion we'll forever own.

In the stillness of the night, I feel your delicate touch

Whispers of eternity, I love you so much.

Your eyes are like stars that glow up the sky above

In your arms, I've found my home, enveloped in your love.

So here I stand, with my heart in my hands

I'm dreaming to tell you, my love never ends.

In every whisper, in every touch

I'm hopelessly devoted, I adore you so much.

Every moment with you is a sweet melody

In your embrace, I find my perfect harmony.

With every breath, I breathe your name

In your arms, forever, I'll remain.

With every breath, your essence fills the air,

A melody of love beyond compare,

My utopia found in your tender care,

A bond so deep, so true, so rare

With you by my side, I am free

In your arms, where I long to be

Together we'll walk, hand in hand

In this paradise, where love will stand.

Your touch sets my soul on fire, like a blazing flame

Dissolving my fears, easing my pain.

Your love is a sweet serenade, that I'll always proclaim

In your eyes, I see forever, our love will remain.

The yearning seemed senseless until my eyes fell on you

Now, my heart beats for you, my love, forever true.

Your love is my obsession

A sweet, intoxicating affliction

I can't oppose the way you make me feel

In your essence, my heart's set free to heal.

Every moment I spend with you
It's like a dream that has come true.
Your touch, your smile, your tender embrace
It brings me to a serene and peaceful place.

Sagas of eternity, our love will never wither
In each other's embrace, our souls are serenely reeled.
Perpetually and invariably, you and I, hand in hand
In this love so true, together we'll stand.

I know, you know, we know,
We have a bond beyond what we describe.
It doesn't need words,
Our actions and eyes speak enough.
They tell the deepest of our mysteries,
Perhaps we never knew about ourselves
But now we know most of it.

It just happened
Unknowingly,
Unexpectedly,
And

Randomly.

All I know is,

I have the memories.

I have you,

I have the past where we enjoyed and cried,

I have the present where we do all silly things

And I manifest to have a future with you too

For better or for worse,

I want to be tied with you

With the red string

No matter what the fate brings.

***

Sea Shore

Come and go

Touch and leave

Your steps are slow.

Express or confess

By words and gestures.

The choice is yours.

I'm waiting

Just the way

I used to do

No matter,

How long it takes.

I'll keep waiting

Just the way shore,

Waits for the waves.

Hoping you'll come

Just like how waves

Comes to the seashore.

***

Addiction of Love

So that's how falling in love feels

Reading our texts with giggles and squeals

The soft pink tint crept on my cheeks

My heart's beating fast, it got me in my feels

He's my baby, ride or die, for real

Addicted to him like a fucking thrill

Loving him's like poppin' a pill

He's a timeless doozy, no dispute

His love made me feel huge

In this ruthless game, he's my fate

Together we conquer, no debate

I'll make him king, there's no time to wait

Flexin' with him, we'll both elevate

Head spinning like a merry-go-round

Lost in his love, can't be found

Addicted to him, I can't come down

In this romance, we hold the crown

He's my muse, my only sound

In the world of love, we have profound

He's my addiction, my drug of choice
His love made me feel like I'm a boss
Can't get enough, no matter the cost
In this love game, he's the sauce
Together we shine, no need to pause
In this raw love, we never lost

Love's raw addict, yeah, that's me
He's my king, I'll make him see
Addicted to his love, I can't break free
In this cruel world, it's just us three
Me, him, and the love that will be
This love's raw, but we are alive and free

Addicted to his touch, like a dope fiend in the streets,
He's my drug of choice, getting me weak in the knees
I can't resist his charm, he got me hypnotised and dazed
Love's a battlefield, it made me feel crazed

We ride or die, baby, ain't no counterfeit
In his eyes, I see the truth, no disguise
Together we're unstoppable, reaching for the skies
Together we shimmer, ain't wasting no time.

I can't believe I'm in love,

Insanely in love with him.

It feels like forever, baby,

It's so true. It's so crazy.

***

Unspoken

Fingers typed a brief message
Both explained their love for each other
How much she meant to him
How much his love caresses her soul.

She typed by her side,
He did the same with his
But then,
Fingers stopped after a point,
Staring at the name above
A thought ran through their minds
And that was it.

Their love remained silent
Their passion remained hidden
And love stated unspoken.

***

All over, Once again

Oh, that white dress
Hugging your body so fine
Oh, your pretty eyes
Stealing my heart with its shine.

All over
Once again.

Your beauty
Shimmered like diamond
You got the elegance of a goddess
Whom I worship with fond.

All over
Once again.

You stood in front of me
Having that toothy smile
My head bowed down with respect
And a dream of you walking down our aisle.

All over
Once again.

"May I?"
I asked, hiding my nervousness
"Sure,"
You spoke with all sweetness.
We held each other
Not wanting to ever let go,
Our eyes talked
With calmness and heartbeats at low.

All over
Once again.

That music playing behind
Added elegance to your pride
I surrendered myself
Except for your shadow,
I have no place to hide.

All over
Once again.

"You look so charming,"
She spoke with utter fondness

"Still your deist,"
I spoke, increasing our closeness.

All over
Once again.

The moonlight showered us with beauty
But she filled me with love
The gods showered us with our needs
But she gave me eternal support.

All over
Once again.

Yes, it was our first dance
In the divine nature
Under the luna's beam
With a calming breeze.
God gave us the blessings
And love rushed through our bodies.

Actually,
With her,
It never felt like the first
Cause I sensed
We shared a beautiful story
Way back before this one took birth.

We looked into each other's eyes,
Promising what we had within
A smile crept over our lips
And our heads joined,
Welcoming the gorgeous future in.

"I love you, wifey," I spoke
Her breaths immediately hitched
A red tint covered her cheeks
Head down with a small smile.

All over
Once again.

"I love you, wifey," I spoke again,

Letting her know, she had my everything evermore

I felt her leaning against me,

Our faces had a negligible gap

"I love you more, my forever,"

She spoke breathily.

All over

Once again.

I knew that dance

was immortally ravishing

in our hearts

Just like other memories

It will be tattooed in our core

as an exquisite art.

Cause we fell in love

in that night

At that very moment

All over

Once again.

***

Paper Rings

I don't need you to

Bring flowers

Write letters

Do all the things

They show in movies.

I don't need you to,

To be loud for me

Show off things

Create those scenarios

They show in movies.

I just need you

To be courageous

To be expressive

To let me know

How you feel.

Let me know
What we hold within us,
Between us.
Cause' I'm all ready
To have us together in
Simple paper rings.

***

Intoxicated Night

She looked like an angel
Maybe that missing piece
I craved for these years.

Her eyes had moisture,
Her fingers grasping the glass.
The breeze running calmly,
While we seated above the cold grass.

The moon must have envied
The moment god gave its aura
To the lady in front of me.

For sure she was much more than words
Beyond the nature's every rule
Yes, I held that beauty of her
In our eternal love pool.

Her smile never left her delicate lips
Neither my heart controlled its beats
Nor that wine affected the boundaries
of our love peaks.

We talked and talked

I learn about her more and more

My eyes stared at her shiny aura

And I let myself sink deeply for her once more.

She carried the life's happiness

While I had only seen the dark

She was carved with fortune

While I suffered the brutal past.

Her lips sipped once again

Giggling and smiling

Hand intertwined with mine

Our love spreading in the surrounding.

Her hands opened side to side

As I watched her standing

She held the bottle of red wine in one

While the other had her heels.

The moon showered his respect and adoration

With its captivating beam

She looked like that moon princess

Mentioned in those stories
She danced, she sang
She talked to those stars
To the moon too,

And my goodness,
I fell in love all over
Once again.

Her inner child intoxicated me once again
Got me smiling ear to ear
Her cheerful voice sang her favourite song
While I thanked god for sending me her
Cause', with her, I won over all my fears.

Yes, she was drunk
Yes, I was drunk
But I swear, that wine was nothing
All we had was, the intoxication of our love.

***

Autumn Night

Beneath the golden leaves, where whispers softly sway,
I found your hand in mine, as twilight kissed the day.
With every drop of rain that slipped, our hearts started to sing,
A hymn of passion that only autumn can bring.

We twirled beneath the grey skies,
Reeling fantasies like threads of gold,
In this dance of precious submission,
We let our sagas unfold.

So let it shower on us tonight,
Let the world wither away,
With every kiss and promise we make,
In this flawless ballet.
The aisle is lined with memories
Our rings are made of adoration and trust,
In the autumn's temperate heartbeat,
It's just you, me and us.

The echoes of our laughter blend
With raindrops on the ground,
In each puddle's reflection lies
An assurance we have found.

We'll build a life from these moments
A tapestry so fine,
As leaves fall like confetti for this love
That's truly divine.

We'll preserve this moment,
Our hearts are eternally secured.
Through seasons varying swiftly
The shades may turn and revolve
But through every turbulent midnight
Love's flame will brightly burn.

Every phase feels so light
When I'm dancing by your side,
Through all seasons
You're my home and my guide.

***

Love can't be defined

Love can't be defined — they say it.

But I can define it.

A word of three letters is enough

To describe what love means to me.

Can you take a guess?

I guess I've made it quite obvious.

And if you connect the dots,

You'll find the answers to all those questions

You always ask me about love.

But I think,

You won't be able to guess it,

Cause' even if I was obvious,

Everything was hidden

Beneath your overthinking.

I hate to admit how introverted am I as a person,

Because whenever I decided to confess,

My anxiety and my self-doubts put barriers.

They say love is indescribable.
But how do I tell them,

I have found what love means.
I have found how love is defined.
I found my definition.

It was HER.
For me, it was HER.
It was YOU.

You — who always ask me if I ever fall in love,
What type of girl would be my partner?
You — who always tease me after I confessed I love
someone.
You — who always motivates me to take a lead
And confess my feelings to that someone.

Little did you know,
That someone was none other than,
You.

Love can't be defined? Nah.

It's a lie.

Ask my friends how my cheeks turn red

Whenever they tease me with your name.

Ask them how the slightest mention of you

Makes me fully alert.

Ask them how I daydream about you

And our moments with an idiotic smile.

Ask them how tense I become whenever

I get to know you're hurt.

I was carefree,

I was avoidant,

I didn't bother to know

What love was?

How it happens?

I found it rubbish.

But then, I found you.

We argued in the first meeting,

Taunted each other in the second.

Got irritated whenever others
Shipped our names together.

A bold girl irritated me.
Her choice of music annoyed me.
Her attitude bugged me.
But then slowly,
Everything about her became precious to me.
I found myself wondering about her.
It was weird when I realized,
what was I doing.

Slowly-slowly, this carefree guy started to care.
Slowly-slowly, the guy who never bothered to even bother,
started to bother whenever he heard something bad happening
to her.
Slowly-slowly, he started listening to the genre of songs she
liked.
Slowly-slowly, he took the initiative to become her friend.
Slowly-slowly, she became his closest friend.

And then slowly-slowly,

He fell in love.

In love with her.

In love with you.

I was naive when you asked me who I love,

And I said your name without even thinking twice.

That's what best friends would do?

I was naive when you asked me what kind of girl pulls my

attention,

And I said your name without any doubt.

I was naive when I explained why a girl like you would be my

partner.

Now when I recall all those moments,

I realize, all this time, I just described you.

The only difference was,

We both considered it a joke.

I was unaware of my own feelings

Yet, my subconscious never failed to express it.

Subconsciously, I always showed care,

I always expressed how much you mean to me
'More than friends'.

'Love'
I hated this word?
I mean I never cared about it much.
But ever since I realized I love you,
This word became my favourite.
And this word became my identity
In front of my friends, our friends
Because they witnessed the change in me.

A change I never opposed or rebelled.
A change that I welcomed so smoothly
That I never comprehended.

Now, let's come back to the point.

I define love,
The way you are,
The way you laugh,
The way you care,
The way you share,
The way you smile,

The way you shine.

The way you bring colours and shimmers with your presence.

The way you console others' wounds and take care of them.

The way you put efforts towards us. Towards me.

You say love isn't for you.

Are you sure, love?

I saved your name with it.

In my contacts,

In my heart,

In my life.

Love can't be defined?

If you still think the same,

Read it all again,

And still, if you can't change your mind,

I'm ready to describe more.

Cause' I can define love,

I can tell what love is for me.

And I'm ready to repeat.

Once?

Twice?

A thousand times.

You ask,

I'll answer.

Love can't be defined — you say.

I'll define it all the way.

And let you know what my love looks like.

It's alive,

It's refreshing,

It's comforting,

It's caring,

It's glazing,

It's beautiful,

It's pretty.

Just the way it is.

And now, change that 'it'

To 'she'.

I defined it. It's HER. It's YOU.

***

I Reside

I may not be with you till the very end,
But you must know where I reside.

I reside in your chest, where your heart beats,
I reside in your every breath.

I reside in all those dreams your eyes see when you sleep,
I reside in your heart-touching voice and your eyes,
I reside in your gaze, which always loved to stare at me with
adoration,
I reside in your smile.

I reside in all of your habits and all of your hobbies,
I reside in your pictures where you stood alone,
I reside in those portraits where we stood together,
I reside in you, my love.

So, make sure you take care of yourself very well,
Just as you used to take care of me.
I remember you once told me possessively that,
You don't like when I get ill.

It hurts you.

So when I reside in you,

Will you take care of me just like before?

I know I said I reside in you.

But still, if you miss me, stare at the sky,

I'll be there with the sun,

Spreading with that sunlight in all the sky.

I'll be in your surroundings

With the birds chirping,

The breeze flowing and the calming smell of nature.

I'll be there in your daily life activities,

And when the day ends,

Just stare at the moon,

The moonlight is me kissing your skin.

I'll come with rain,

Touching every essence of yours.

Just in case, you miss any of these,

Just know I said I reside in you,

So put your hand on your chest and close your eyes,

And feel the beats. They're my words.

I reside in your soul.

I reside in all those places where you go.

I reside in those handwritten letters we wrote.

I reside in memories we made

And I reside in the man I loved wholeheartedly.

I mean my words. I reside in you.

***

A Beautiful Canto

He was a beautiful canto,
Incomplete yet so complete
Something precious to hold onto.
Maybe I got enough stanzas
To express the beautiful phase.

A perfect poetry,
A perfect tune
Maybe perfect words,
But finest memories.

The start was uncertain
None of us knew
And none of us was to blame.
It's still fascinating
How these verses were written.
All I know
All I remember
Is,
I was smitten.

Began with the symphony
Of friendship we were unaware of.
Instant connection was there
No hesitation, no nervousness
The music sounded like a dove.

Notes hit in a rhythm,
A deep meaning of each
Carved in my memory.

An unknown resonance entered
And I understood what it meant,
The jealousy I started to have.
Whenever I saw him closely talking
To other girls,
There was a part of my heart
That felt a sharp pang.
But maybe,
That was a common overrated slang?

It felt weird.

It wasn't like
I didn't have crush on anyone before
But none of them felt like
The way this one did.

This became a distinct feature
Of that verse.

Uncertainty created a beautiful mess
The unknown resonance seemed
To be at peace.
The tension in my heart seemed to cease.
Though my insecurities were there to ruin it all,
I overcame it nevertheless.
I won over every insecurity
With his invisible help
Of what he was unknown about.

The time passed,
And now,
A beautiful harmony started to occur.

A melody so powerful and sweet
Lyrics for the verse were blurry in my mind
My behaviour and words started to cheat
Where everyone knew,
It was one of a kind.

The stanzas till now
Suddenly turned into notable
Each word and line was clear
Yet we kept the things without any label.
Well, did we need the label?

No.
In my opinion,
We never did,
And if we did somewhere,
In parallel universe
Then fate must have had
Something to keep hidden
As a reason, for taking our care.

But now,

Back to the time,

I had seen beautiful phases.

Strangers to friends,

Friends to crushes,

Crushes to…

Well,

If I look back at all of those now,

I can conclude him as my first love.

Why?

Every time this love happens,

It brings massive emotional rides,

The urge to ride or die,

Every moment, every word exchanged,

Jealousy and insecurities,

Assurance and bond,

And everything I'm not able to remember right now.

For me,

He brought that phase.

Not only did he bring it up,

He lived it out with me,

Probably only in the form of

Some mere crush of his

But he did.

Even after all this time,

The words are still incomplete for that chapter,

The music remained unreleased,

Lyrics never got fully disclosed

Yet,

It gave birth to a masterpiece

An incomplete one

But still so complete on its own way.

He was,

He'd be,

As always,

A forever beautiful canto

In my heart

And my life.

***

Muse

I can taste you in all those memories
And your laughs in each.
Every eye contact we had,
My deepest secrets were revealed.
Every smile we shared.
Tattooed an aesthetic vibe
Insecurities flew above in the sky
Like a free wild kite.

I was scared,
What if,
You'll know the secrets
I've never told anyone before?
But you made it so easy
For me to lose it all.
I was the impatient wave
And you were the calming shore
Silencing the restlessness in my core.
Never knew that
A beautiful picture will emerge from blues.
And get filled with different hues.

I wrote every emotion
I felt at that time,
In every moment,
Penned down what my feelings were
For you back then.

You knew pen and paper were my friends
And you never held me back,
You knew you were my muse
And you never got fused.
And as I got to know it,
I was flustered and amused.

I had stopped writing my emotions
But you pushed me to start it again,
It was my first time
Tasting the sweet love potions.
With a lot of gain and some beautiful pain.

You knew you were muse
But you never put this confession in your misuse.

And I fell for it even more,

That people were afraid sayin'

I won't be able to move on.

But,

Was it wrong to write down

About those feelings

I comprehend will never be gone?

You brought the best in me

The different layers of mine

That I always hide, were finally free.

Each of them felt relieved

To come out and express,

You came and caressed

The stir in me.

They'll say it always

And perhaps I'll let them too,

But no one could change it ever,

You were my muse.

A muse that could never be forgotten,

That could never feel boring.

***

My Last Favour

In the fragments I fell on the ground

I saw myself being broken

And shattered around,

The pieces of my hopes and dreams

Busted and deeply drowned.

The walls I built,

The dreams I had woven

Of us,

Of our future,

Everything disappeared

Like they never had a trace.

My last favour,

For your love

My heart, a jigsaw,

No longer stayed whole.

But still,

I held onto some fading echoes

With all my might,

To the hope that was left

The light that felt right.

I shone in the darkness
Even if it meant to burn myself
To lit every single hope within us,
Even if it meant to give myself
To you, even if it meant only for lust.

I crumbled, I cried
I begged you to hug me,
To give me another false hope
So I could stay.

I'm breaking down
Still inside my memory,
The future outside
A blur, a haze,
My future, so uncertain,
My past, a daze.

My last favour,
For your love,
I kept all the good memories above,
Just to convince myself, we were good.

I was so blind

To believe all of your lies,

To let you make me find,

Never existing happiness and prize.

Now when I look back,

It didn't make any sense.

This was when I understood,

I was trapped in one-sided love

So dense.

And now,

When I'm trying to pick up

Every broken piece and join them,

I see you standing at my door

In a stormy, rainy night.

Telling me that you love me still,

That there's still a hope for you to fill

All the voids, and that I shouldn't fight.

How dare you to have that audacity?

After tearing everything apart?

My last favour
For your love,
I'll not fight myself
To keep good memories of you,
To keep our first kiss in my mind
To keep all those moments
When you meant you loved me.

But,
I have decided to let go.
To treat myself better,
To let myself overcome
Every pain you gave.
With this in my mind,
I'm ending our small letter.

I have seen myself broken
My strength getting depleted
My spirit all weary
With my will turning like astray.

My steps are surely unsure now,

And my path's unclear today.

But this time, I'd overcome all

And never let myself at bay.

My last favour,

For your love

A final gift to leave my heart's desire,

And set our love on fire.

Oh, my last favour,

For your love,

I choose myself

To cherish and to love.

***

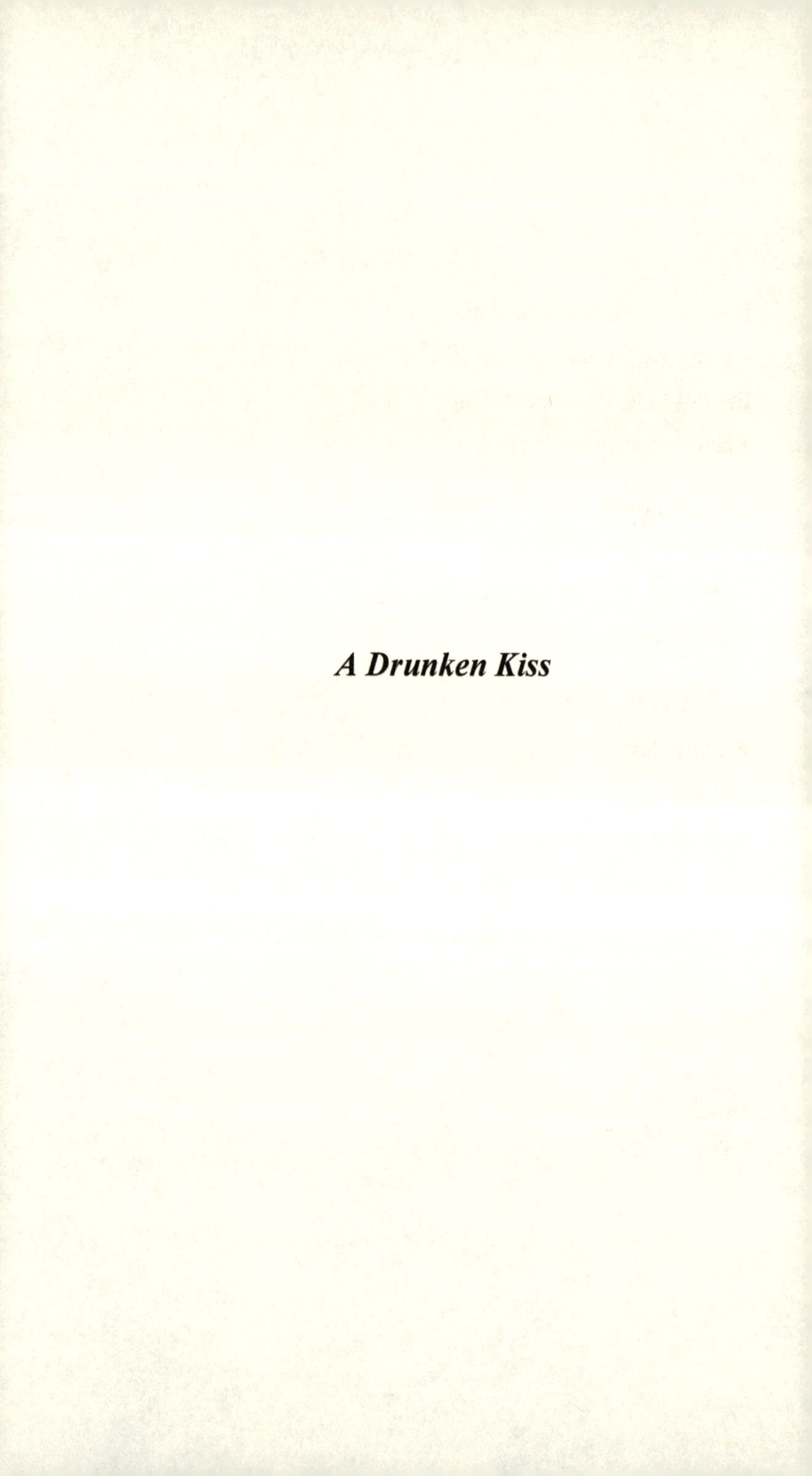

A Drunken Kiss

We were in a restaurant,
With your friends and mine,
Having snacks with lots of beer
And wine.

My eyes were fixated on you
The way you got along with everyone,
And I was trying to not be silent
As always.

I was an introverted bird,
Never spoke much,
And never continued
If someone interrupted.
But you were there to listen,
To make sure I wasn't left out,
To make others hear me too.
You were like the guy
Straight out of those romance fictions.

Tonight you were shining
Maybe my friends observed my
fond staring,
And perhaps they also knew
What my heart was hiding.

I was an introverted girl,
It was obvious that
My lips never spoke my confession.
But my eyes do.
But, I was never a brave one
to make an eye contact with you.

These talks weren't helping either
All about crushes and love.
And I could sense your gaze on me
Perhaps you were curious if I had any.

None of us didn't realise
when the evening turned into night
while we were talking,
And it was time to go home.

I was drunk

Not in my senses

But I felt a pair of arms

lifting me up and carrying

me to a car.

I moved my hazy vision

Only to see and realize

It's you who's carrying.

Maybe it was a taxi

I saw the yellow colour.

You sat inside with me

in your arms,

My eyes looking at you,

Observing your ethereal

facial charms.

And I wondered

What if I say it out loud?

What if I tell you I love you?

You might haven't expected

Nor imagined.

And I was scared,
What if this confession
would lead to an end
that I feared?
Or to a new start
I dreamt of.

I wondered if you ever
felt the emotions I'm having,
I wondered if you ever
observed my silly hints,
I wondered if you noticed
my shyness around you,
And I wondered a million
more questions all the time.

You have a personality
that pulled me in like a magnetic,
You have a voice
that hypnotized me,
You have a warmth
that caressed my soul.

You have everything
that made me fall for you
without my permission,
But I don't complain.
I liked that feeling.

I don't know how to
When to,
With what words,
I should confess to you.
I'm nervous,
I'm scared,
What if things don't go well?
But to know that too,
I had to say it to you.
That's what I discovered,
And that's what I heard
from my friends.

I gently kept my hand on your cheek,
Causing you to look at me confusedly.

My body shivered slightly,
As I felt my heart thudding restlessly.

I balanced a bit
And leaned in,
And let my heart take the charge.
My eyes closed and lips touched yours,
You stayed still
But I kept our lips touched.

I know you'd think
It's the alcohol,
And I don't care.
I know I may forget it tomorrow
And I don't care.

The drunken kiss I initiated
I planned to pour my love
for you in it.
But the last thing I could remember
You kissed back eventually.
Was it a yes? Or just alcohol's heat?

Thank You

So recently I realized,

I don't love you anymore

Your name doesn't excite me

And that I don't even like you anymore.

I used to be silly and insane,

Had emotions I couldn't explain.

My expectations and hopes

for future,

Survived through suture.

The phase was a roller-coaster ride,

Had many days and nights where I

cried.

But I don't complain,

I learnt from them,

None of it all went in vain.

So thank you for everything,

For every memory

And every laughter,

For every tear,

For every talk,

Even for my insecurities.

I'm over you now,

But I'll never stop appreciating

these moments.

Maybe no one would understand

why would I keep cherishing them,

And treating them like diamonds.

I may hear, 'move on'

'Don't stay stuck' phrases,

But I'd still be grateful for you

To give me one of the precious

chapters.

So thank you.

***

...

I hate the way

I hate the way you stimulate emotions within me that I once found cringe-worthy and utterly foreign to my being.

The air between us is thick with a tension that is both electric and implicit, creating an atmosphere that seems to vibrate with our unacknowledged feelings. The mere sight of you sends a jolt of energy through my veins, igniting a fire that I had long believed was extinguished. Yet, this flame now burns with an intensity I never anticipated, illuminating aspects of myself I thought I had safely hidden away.

I can't help but be pulled toward you, like a moth irresistibly drawn to a flickering candle, even though my mind echoes warnings against such recklessness. The emotions you evoke in me are both thrilling and terrifying, a bewildering rollercoaster ride—one that I can't seem to master or navigate.

When I'm with you, I find myself exploring thoughts and desires that I once considered unacceptable, or even shameful. You have a unique way of challenging my deeply held beliefs and pushing me beyond the boundaries I've carefully crafted around myself. It's a terrifying dance of exhilaration and insecurity that spins my world off its axis.

I loathe the way you peel back the layers of my constructed persona, revealing the raw and vulnerable core of who I genuinely am. It's as if you possess a key—a special insight that unlocks the most secret, guarded chambers of my soul. This unveiling leaves me feeling starkly exposed and unprotected, echoing a mixture of dread and helplessness.

Despite my fervent wish to maintain my distance, I feel an undeniable pull toward you. It's a force that transcends logic, drawing me closer in a way I never thought possible. I find myself craving your touch, your gaze, your very essence in a manner that seems irrational yet profoundly real.

The emotional landscape you create is both exhilarating and disorienting; one moment, I'm soaring high on the wings of your affection, buoyed by a sense of joy and connection that feels almost euphoric. However, in the next heartbeat, I plummet into the murky depths of self-doubt and insecurity, battling a tempest within me.

I hate the way you push my boundaries, forcing me to confront feelings I thought I had mastered, drying up the wells of certainty I had built around myself. Your influence over me does not just challenge my perceptions; it possesses a certain power—an intoxicating blend of fear and desire that is hard to reconcile.

When I'm with you, I find myself indulging in wild and liberated thoughts, desires that I previously suppressed. These feelings are a dizzying cocktail of elation and dread, leaving me reeling and breathless in their wake.

I hate how you manage to ignite emotions I once scoffed at, unravelling the carefully woven fabric of my identity to expose the raw, unguarded essence that dwells within. You hold a mysterious and potent power over me, one that ignites both a thrilling charge and a haunting vulnerability.

Ultimately, despite my best attempts to resist this magnetic attraction, I find myself drawn to you like a moth to a flame, a dance of risk that defies all reason. The craving for your warmth and presence intensifies within me, revealing depths of longing I never knew existed.

This intricate web of feelings you create is both liberating and terrifying—a whirlwind of emotions that leaves me gasping for composure. One moment I might be elated, soaring on the high of your affection, and the next I'm plummeting into a cavern of self-questioning and unease.

I despise the way you make me confront emotions I once dismissed, challenging my assumptions and propelling me beyond the protective walls I painstakingly erected. Your power over me is evident, sparking that complex interplay of fear and yearning that defines our connection.

In your presence, I find myself caught in the throes of thoughts and desires long suppressed; feelings that feel both reckless and exhilarating. The collision of liberation and fear sends me spinning, each moment a dizzying exploration of what it means to be truly vulnerable.

I…

'I hate the way I fell for you because of these cringy things I used to tease you with.'

***

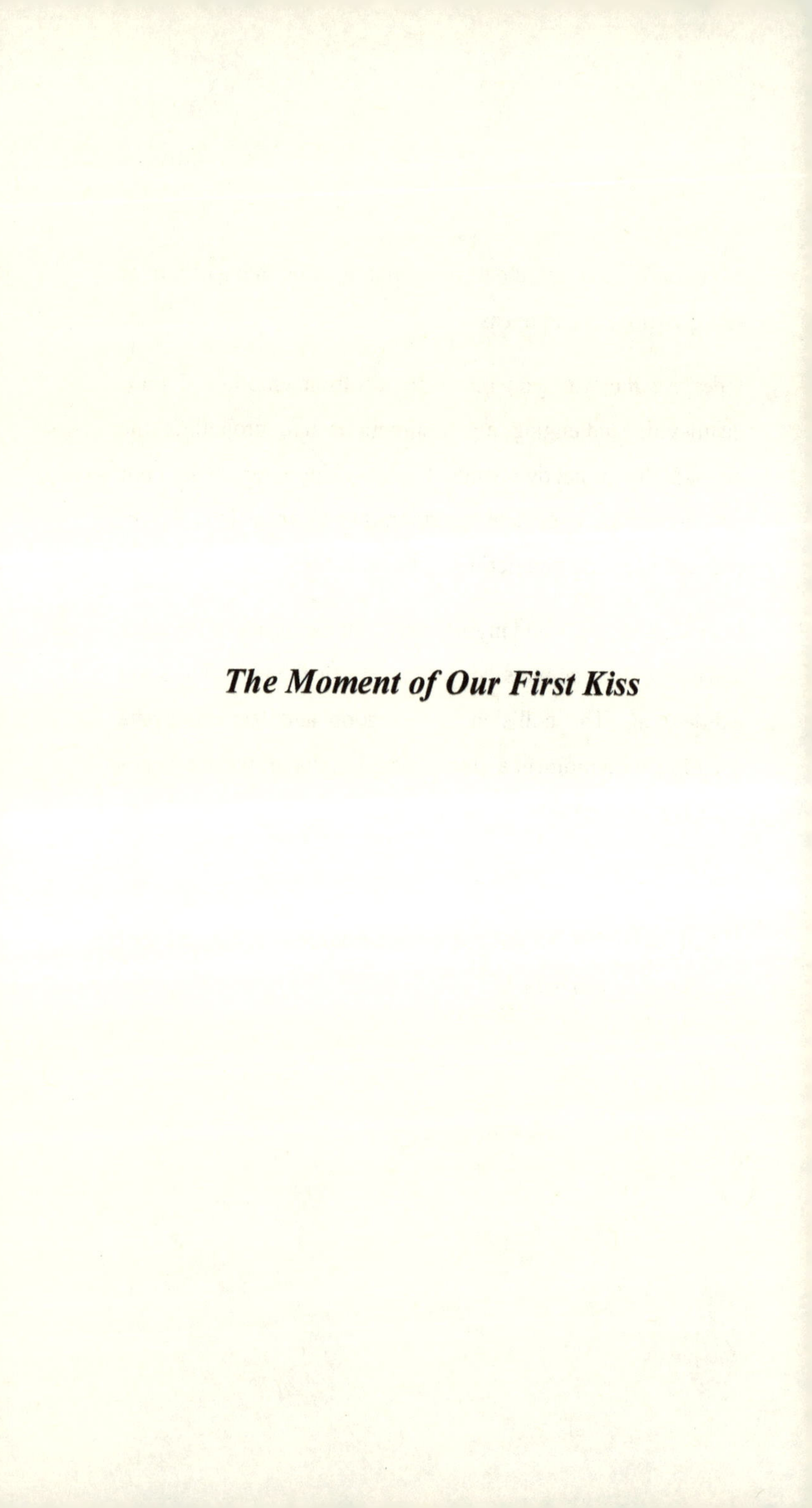

The Moment of Our First Kiss

Under the soft, ethereal glow of the moonlight, we stood enveloped in each other's warmth, our bodies seamlessly intertwined like two vines twining around a sturdy trellis. In that exquisite instant when our lips first brushed against each other, it felt as if a cosmic symphony of emotions erupted, a beautiful dance of fervour and gentleness that transcended the very limits of time and space.

The night was alive with the melodious whispers of the wind, which caressed our skin with a gentle touch, carrying with it the intoxicating scent of blooming flowers that filled the air with sweetness. As we stood there, wrapped in the embrace of one another, the world around us began to dissolve into a hazy backdrop, as if we were the sole two souls in a universe crafted just for us.

Your eyes sparkled with the shimmering reflection of distant stars, mesmerizing me and drawing me deeper into the enigmatic depths of your soul. Within them, I saw a mirror of my own vulnerability and longing, a profound connection that went beyond the physical realm and reached into the very core of our beings.

As our fingers intertwined, an exhilarating spark ignited between us, a fervent blaze that seemed almost ready to engulf us in its intensity. The warmth of your touch sent delightful shivers racing down my spine, awakening every single nerve ending, and rendering me utterly entranced by the electric presence that radiated from you.

The air enveloping us grew thick with anticipation, each breath mingling together in a shared rhythm, each heartbeat echoing the unspoken tension that lingered in the night. As we leaned in, our lips mere inches apart, the world itself appeared to pause, holding its breath in collective anticipation for the moment our lips would finally meet.

And then, in a tender explosion, it happened. Our lips brushed against each other softly at first, a gentle, hesitant exploration of the enchanted unknown. Yet, as time trickled on, that initial brush deepened, evolving into a passionate embrace, as if we were striving to convey an eternity of emotions within that single, electrifying moment.

Time itself seemed to hold still as we surrendered to the embrace, our bodies moulding together like pieces of a long-lost puzzle, our souls intertwining in a breath-taking tapestry of connection. The chaos of the world around us faded to a distant whisper, leaving only the profound bond we shared, an unbreakable link that spiralled beyond the physical into the depths of our hearts.

The kiss transformed into a magnificent symphony of emotions, a crescendo of uncontainable passion and desire that threatened to overwhelm us both. We poured our hearts into that kiss, our bodies swaying in perfect harmony as if the universe had conspired to create a moment where we were meant to find each other again and again.

As we finally pulled apart, breathless and flushed, we locked eyes, a silent understanding blossoming between us. In that moment of deep connection, we recognized that this was more than a fleeting encounter; it was a bond of significance, one that would linger long after the night had faded into dawn.

The air around us crackled with the remnants of our fervent exchange, the lingering scent of our mingled breaths weaving together a tapestry of intimacy and longing. We stood lost in one another's arms, our hearts racing and souls intertwined, cradled in the sanctuary of that sacred night.

The cosmos sprawled above us, its stars glimmering like ancient witnesses to our dance. We swayed to the rhythm of our synchronized heartbeats, where every touch, every whisper, became a note in the grand symphony of love and desire, enveloping us in an exquisite embrace.

As we held each other closer, the outside world faded into the shadows, rendering it insignificant against the vibrant connection we shared. In that transcendent moment, our spirits surged as one, creating a beautiful dance filled with pure, unadulterated passion that left the very fabric of our beings altered forever.

The night transformed into our personal sanctuary, a haven where we could escape the confines of reality and lose ourselves in the resplendent embrace of our love. We revelled in the freedom that ensued, the delightful vulnerability of our souls laid bare for each other in trust and honesty.

Every kiss became a testament to the depth of our emotions, a visceral display of feelings that threatened to consume us whole. We infused every touch, every tender word with the weight of our yearning, striving to express an entire lifetime of love and longing encapsulated in that single, precious moment.

And so, enveloped in the warmth of our love, we surrendered to the magic of the night, discovering anew the unparalleled beauty of the connection we forged. Nothing else mattered but the bond that intertwined our very essences, a love story written among the stars, one that would echo in eternity passion.

***

Love with Eyes

As they began to converse, an air of romance filled the space between them. The smiles they exchanged and the words they shared about anything and everything only intensified this feeling. Yet, in those fleeting moments when their gazes met, something truly magical happened. Her heart began to race, her cheeks flushed with warmth, and his smile widened, revealing a rosy tint that spread across their faces like a sunrise.

As they stood there, love filled their hearts and overtook their senses. She found herself completely entranced by the depth of his eyes as if they were a window into his soul. Every time she looked into them, she felt herself sinking deeper and deeper, unable to look away. Meanwhile, he couldn't help but notice how her eyes sparkled when she laughed, or how her smile lit up the room. He marvelled at the way she moved and spoke, captivated by her every gesture. Love had truly enveloped them both, and they were lost in the enchantment of each other's presence.

"Does he even know what he has done to me?" she often thought as she stared at him.

"I wish I could explain my feelings to her; it's just that the words in my mind are so jumbled that I don't know where to start," he always confessed, though he kept it unspoken.

The way their eyes met spoke volumes, telling a story that their lips could never fully convey. Every time she looked at him, she felt herself being drawn in deeper, and in his heart, he felt the same. They found themselves in an endless cycle of falling for each other again and again, yet they both remained curious about how much deeper their love could go. Their unspoken connection was palpable as if every glance and touch said more than words ever could. But still, they couldn't help but wonder whether they should express their love through words or actions.

It burned her heart when she saw him talking to another girl. He sensed that same burning sensation in his heart when he noticed her giggling with another guy.

"It's just that I cannot stop. It's just that I cannot even let you know," she always whispered to herself while sitting in the corner, watching him.

"I wish I could kiss you here and let everyone know that you are mine, but I guess I still don't have the courage. I am still not brave enough," he often said to his heart, staring at her with emotions he wished he could explain.

Their love story began with the depth of her eyes and the way he worshipped her gaze. Staring into each other's eyes was their love language, a promise to sink deeper into their connection. Unspoken words lingered between them, kept hidden by their jealousy. They expressed their love through gestures, too shy to show it any other way. For them, love through their eyes embodied their promise, commitment, and devotion.

***

Confessing to You

I don't know what to say; things have been complicated. Your hands are intertwined with mine, and I am becoming intoxicated by your eyes, like old wine. You must have sensed that things were different today; maybe our silence made it obvious.

I am unsure whether it would be right or not, but they say not to fall in love with your friend, as it may lead to heartbreak. He might reveal the truth to you or play along, depending on what he wants, considering your goodness.

I keep staring at your silent figure before me, watching me with curiosity, unawareness, and perhaps excitement. My lips long to express how much I hate it when you sit with her and talk. I wish I could explain how jealous I feel, and how much I want my voice to rise and declare to the world that you are mine. I wish you could understand that I have cried because of the insecurities that overwhelm me when you are with her.

I know she is just a friend; there is nothing else between them. But these feelings are not intentional. My heart burns with anguish, piercing my soul into pieces. To you, she may be a friend, but I have given you my heart and love. That heart can't bear the thought of you being with someone else. I wish I were courageous enough to express my feelings to you.

Finally, I took a deep breath, looking down for a moment before meeting your deep gaze again. "I love you," I finally managed to say, though it seemed to leave your face untouched by emotion. I know how much anxiety I carry. "This is a mutual feeling," you replied. Maybe you couldn't say it back like everyone else, but that word—'mutual'—transported me to a world of dreams where I imagined a paradise with you.

Your face remained calm and unbothered, and your voice was deeper than the Pacific Ocean. We just stared into each other's eyes until I felt myself leaning in and kissing your lips, a small smile forming between us.

***

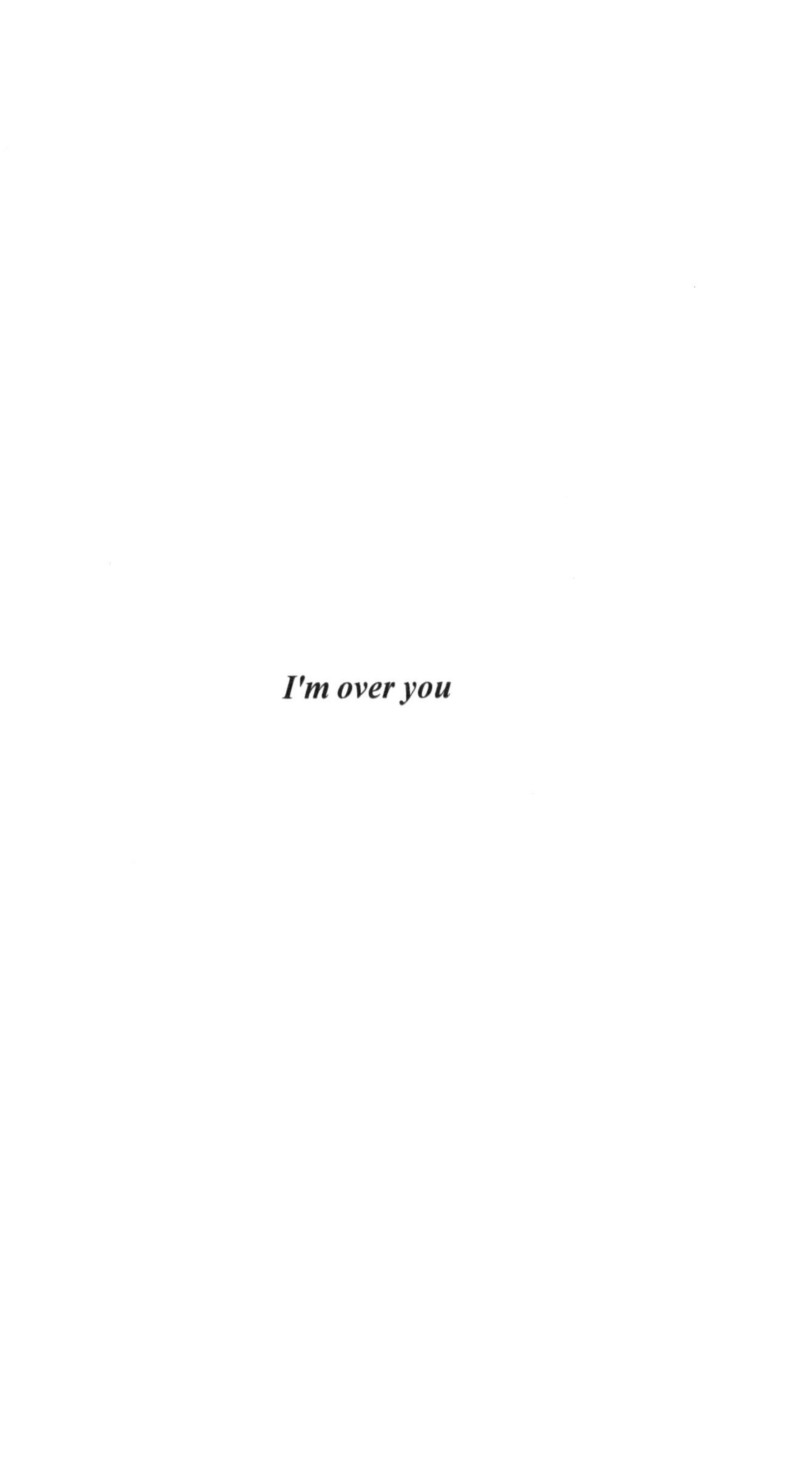

I'm over you

I was talking to one of my friends today, and she teased me by mentioning your name. I realized that it no longer makes my heart flutter like it used to; it doesn't give me butterflies in my stomach anymore. In the past, every conversation we had brought me a unique kind of happiness, excitement, and warmth that seemed to chase away all my negative emotions, even if just for a little while.

In the past, I longed to hear your voice and often wished I could talk to you. Each time I called, I felt a strange restlessness. When you answered, my heart would race, thudding loudly in my chest. Those calls would leave me with sweet memories that lingered for a long time.

For some time now, as I reflect on these memories, I find myself wondering what happened to me. When I stood in front of you, I know I must have seemed different—overly emotional, maybe foolish, and at times quite bold. You might have questioned some of my actions at certain points, and I wouldn't be surprised if that crossed your mind.

I admit there was something; something magical in those moments when I realized I had feelings for you. Something about it made me feel deeply attached to you. I wanted to share everything with you—my secrets, fears, and everything in between. I found myself waiting for your messages, looking for you in class, and when I saw you sitting with another girl, I couldn't help but feel a twinge of jealousy too.

Those memories are still fresh today. But now they are also dull somewhere. Earlier, I used to feel so happy just listening to your name. I excitedly used to tell my friends about the moments I shared with you.

It's not like I never had any insecurities. I had insecurities that weighed heavily on me. I would often cry in front of you and even our friends, but I could never find a way to express what I was feeling. At that time, I didn't even know how to communicate those emotions.

Even after our confession, we chose to remain friends, and we understand why. Nevertheless, I often wonder and hope for a future chance together. What if we had an opportunity later on?

I always wished that something would happen; something that would bring us together in the way I desired. That desire raised my expectations too high. But nothing happened, and even after I learned the truth, it hurt badly.

As I look back on those moments, I can't help but feel that what I experienced with you was akin to the infamous first love that so many people talk about. They often mention that this magical encounter usually happens in your late teens, when emotions run high and everything feels more intense. Perhaps you were that for me. Perhaps, you were my first love.

They describe it as an electrifying connection that sparks, a pull so strong it feels as if the very air around you both is charged with energy. An undeniable chemistry, a deep-seated attraction that resonates through every glance and touch. It is as though a swarm of butterflies danced in your stomach, each flutter igniting a warmth that spreads throughout your entire being. The euphoria is intoxicating, a bright tide of joy that swirls around you, envelops you in a blissful haze. And in every moment we shared, I experienced all of this with you. There was a profound euphoria that enveloped me, as though I was walking on air.

These things were of those days. Now things are different.

I no longer miss you. Your name doesn't excite me the way it used to. The butterflies I once felt are gone now. My heart doesn't long to talk to you anymore. It took me almost two years to realize that you have become just a phase for me, much like the beautiful memories of childhood. They happen only once and are often recalled at random.

I may smile as I talk about it, and I might seem happy, but that's because I truly cherish that time in my life. I hope my fondness for it doesn't lead to a feeling of being stuck or not moving on. After all, cherishing a beautiful phase of your life isn't a bad thing, right? I enjoyed every moment while it lasted. Even though there were some painful experiences, I appreciate them because they contributed to who I am today. I learned valuable lessons and had important experiences, and that's what truly matters.

Some of my friends often tell me to move on whenever I discuss this phase of my life, thinking I'm stuck. Maybe they don't believe that I've moved on, even when I assure them I have. I can't change their perspective, but I do appreciate their concern.

I discovered profound insights about love, delved into the rich tapestry of emotions that enveloped me in those fleeting moments with you. The feelings were intense and beautiful, creating a vivid memory that lingers in my heart. I am truly grateful for this experience and the cherished memories it has left me with.

I want to express my heartfelt gratitude for the precious moments we shared. I cherish those late nights when we poured our hearts out through texts, revealing our innermost thoughts and feelings. I deeply appreciate the conversations that went beyond the surface, where we connected on a profound level, exchanging dreams, fears, and hopes. Thank you for being a part of those unforgettable moments that will always hold a special place in my heart. Thank you for sharing such a meaningful chapter in my life.

Although I don't think I need to, but I think I should say it for one last time —

'I'm over you.'

***

Something I'd like to share with you all

It's truly fascinating how words can become both our sweetest and strongest weapon for self-expression. Whether woven together in poetry or stories, they have the power to capture our hearts. We learn and grow through our experiences, often critiquing our earlier works, but deep down, we recognize that they conveyed something meaningful. Even if they don't appear as polished as others' creations, they still hold value.

Perhaps that's why they have always held a special charm for me. Each time I immersed myself in a poem or a story, I found myself enchanted, marvelling at the way a writer could craft their thoughts and emotions into words. Whether it was a vivid work of fiction that transported me to another world, an insightful piece of non-fiction that broadened my horizons, or a poignant poem that stirred my heart, every literary encounter only deepened my affection for the transformative power of writing.

I have explored many genres—romance, angst, comedy, and horror—but romance always leaves my heart thrilled. I don't know why, but I have a deep love for romantic stories. Whether they are contemporary, dark, sad, involve second chances, or focus on self-love, the various tropes always provide me with an exhilarating experience.

And that's how I embarked on my journey with words, penning small romantic poems that were inspired by a few pieces I stumbled upon online. Back then, I barely had any understanding of what romance truly meant or the depth of love I was trying to express through my verses. Each poem was a spontaneous outpouring of emotions, crafted during moments of inspiration when my heart felt full. I poured my thoughts onto the page, creating a tapestry of feelings, even if I didn't fully grasp their significance at the time.

I definitely had people who questioned me, saying things like, "What are you even writing? Is it about your age? You're just spoiling yourself." And like any normal child who simply wanted to explore and try new things, I was shushed. As a result, I stopped writing for a while. However, I was inspired to return to writing after I started listening to audiobooks and reading fan fiction. This time, I not only wrote poetry but also began crafting stories.

I began exploring various romance genres again, realizing that my fascination with them had never faded. I started writing simple stories about sad love, where one character dies at the end while the other lives on for them, or tales of two people falling in love and living happily together, among others. I can't even remember where those stories are now—maybe I deleted them. However, this time I gained exposure to many aspects of life and love, and found the story of first love. I'm grateful that it happened, as it provided me with a wealth of inspiration, leading me to write poetry and stories based on those experiences.

I realize that I cannot constantly draw upon those memories to fuel my creativity, as repeating them would result in echoes of my past work. I want to avoid that at all costs. Perhaps this book represents a turning point, signalling the conclusion of my exploration of the emotions intertwined with those cherished memories. I hope that as you read, you will not only feel but vividly envision the moments I have tenaciously tried to weave into words, bringing to life the depth and richness of my experiences.

This book includes not only poems but also some short, diary-like stories. I'm not quite sure how to define those sections or what to call them. It features poems based on real-life experiences, as well as pieces that are purely imaginative.

I hope you enjoy the woven words in this book and that it resonates with your emotions as well. Please let me know your thoughts! You can connect with me on Instagram; my username is @authorpradeeptiranjan.

Thank you and lots of love. Take care.